More Techniques
of
Beading Earrings

Book II

by

Deon DeLange

Eagle's View Publishing
A WestWind, Inc. Company
6756 North Fork Road
Liberty, UT 84310

Library of Congress Number: 83-82121
ISBN 0-943604-12-5

DeLange, Deon, 1938-
  More techniques of beading earrings : book II
      / by Deon DeLange --
  p. cm.
  ISBN 0-943604-12-5

  1. Beadwork. 2. Earrings. 3. Jewelry making. I. Title

TT860   745.5942
                                      QB190-278

15 14 13 12 11 10 9 8 7 6 5 4

CONTENTS

About the Author

Before writing her first book of **Techniques of Beading Earrings,** Deon had been making and creating beaded earrings and necklaces for twelve years. She has won a number of awards at state fairs, pow wows and craft shows and what started as a personal interest has developed into a family enterprise. Deon's daughter, Yvette, when only eleven years old, starting winning awards for her creative earring designs and many of the designs in this volume were made by her.

In 1982 the family decided to make craftwork a full-time vocation and in 1983, with the encouragement of her family, friends and editor, started writing her first book about making earrings and necklaces with seed beads and other traditional Indian materials. That book was a great success and in answer to those who read and used the first volume and asked for more designs and variations, this book is dedicated with heart felt appreciation.

* * * * * * * * * * * *

Acknowledgments

Deon would like to thank her editor, Monte Smith, for his help in completing this book, his ideas, and his photographic talents. Ralph L. Smith assisted in designing the book and supplied the graphics and illustrations. Ann Cutrubus "proof- read" the manuscript a number of times and made many valuable suggestions. Most important of all, to my husband and children whose encouragement made this all possible.

INTRODUCTION

While every design that appears in this book is new, many of the directions that were in the first volume of **Techniques of Beading Earrings** are repeated herein for the benefit of those who do not have access to the first book in this series and for those who have that book but wish to review this material. Most of the designs and variations that are in the first book are easier to make than those that follow and the person who is just starting to make earrings may want to consult that book before attempting some of the more complicated designs in this one. Still, all the directions needed to create beautiful earrings and necklaces are explained and illustrated in this book and the basic steps are clearly outlined in this introduction and the fundamental designs that follow. The craftsperson who has mastered these techniques may wish to pass over this material and go directly to the new techniques, designs and variations.

Every attempt has been made to make this book easy and enjoyable to use. Following this "Introduction" are complete instructions on making the basic "Deon's Designs Originale" Earrings. This is followed by graphed designs of the basic styles and these start with the easiest earrings and progress to the more difficult designs; all of the designs used are new and even the experienced beadworker will enjoy making the earrings that are graphed out in these examples. The next section is of new and more complicated designs and variations and these build on the techniques explained above, and in the first book, to more difficult styles.

There is then a description of how to make necklaces and necklace chains and then how to make other types of earrings and their variations.

The important thing to remember when using this book is that each of the designs, no matter how difficult, is created from the basic steps that are explained and illustrated at the beginning. When a new variation requires another technique it is explained and that builds to more complicated designs and so forth. It is helpful, therefore, to master the basics first and then each new technique as it is explained.

<<<<<<<<<< * >>>>>>>>>>

Making earrings and necklaces with beads is enjoyable and creative. There are, however, a few things to keep in mind that will help make beading easier and will also be helpful in using this book.

(1) Be selective in choosing beads of uniform size. This is very important in this kind of beadwork in order to obtain a pleasing, over-all appearance and to insure uniformity in design.

The most uniform beads are available from Indian craft supply houses and are purchased in bunches called "hanks." When buying the beads, it is important to place all of the colors to be used side by side and insure that all of the beads are uniform. Each hank, however, will have a number of beads that have weird shapes or are slightly larger or smaller than the others and these should be discarded as the beading is done. If it is necessary to purchase the beads in containers, be very selective when beading to choose uniform beads.

(2) When making any of the earrings that have both bugle beads and seed beads, the size of the bugle bead determines what size seed bead to use. Therefore, a size 3/° bugle bead may be used with size 11/° or 12/° seed beads, but a size 2/° may be used with only size

12/° seed beads or smaller. In all glass seed beads the larger the number the smaller the bead.

(3) Keep the beads in separate containers or jars. This will make finding the needed color and size bead easier and will insure that different sizes do not get mixed. For future work, it may be advisable to not only label the size and color on the containers, but also the color number and where they were purchased. Most craft supply houses have their own color numbers and this will make reordering easier.

(4) Be sure you have enough beads of the proper colors to finish your project before beginning. Bead colors will vary in shade from dye batch to dye batch and it is often impossible to find the right shade when a project is half complete.

(5) When beading, use a felt covered desk blotter or a piece of styrofoam that has been covered with fabric. It is best to have a work area that is comfortable to work on and that will not allow the beads to roll away. As the beading is done, the different colors and sizes of beads should be kept in separate piles, or in different saucers (white is the best color), or trays, or they may be taken directly from the hank strings. The idea is to be able to select uniform beads as you work, so try different methods to find the one that works best for you.

(6) The best needles for this kind of work are made in England and are Size 15/° Beading Needles. If these are unavailable, a size 16/° Japanese beading needle can be used, but these are generally more brittle, larger and less convenient to use.

(7) The best thread to use is "Nymo" (made of nylon), in a size "A" or "0."

(8) Always work in a well lighted room. It may be that a clamp-on elbow lamp or a desk lamp with an adjustable neck will be helpful. However, flouorescent lighting is not suggested, as it tends to alter the color of some beads.

(9) A pair of small pointed, sharp craft scissors will be very helpful. When cutting the

thread from a finished piece of beadwork, lay the scissor blades flat against the beadwork and then clip carefully close to the work. Clipping the threads with just the tips of the blades at an angle could cut threads that are part of the beadwork that should not be cut.

(10) When making necklace and earring sets, try to use complimentary designs that show a relationship between the two. A necklace using floral designs will compliment earrings if they also have similar floral designs, etc.

(11) It is suggested that the beginner use small and simple designs to begin, then progress to larger and more difficult pieces. Making several pairs of earrings in the beginning will help keep away from frustration and mistakes that can occur with larger work.

(12) Please read the complete procedure for making the earring or necklace before beginning the beadwork so that you will have a more complete understanding of the technique.

PLATE I

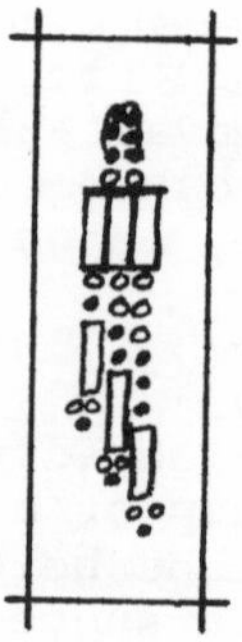

LEGEND

▯ = Brown
    Bugle

○ = Beige
● = Brown

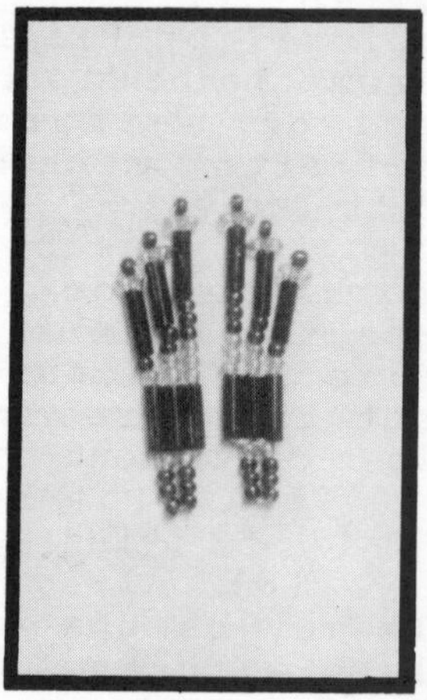

Small TAPERED DANGLE EARRING

DEON'S DESIGNS

ORIGINALE EARRINGS

This first section explains the basic techniques and all of these earrings may be made with the following recommended materials:

    1 bobbin "nymo" thread size A or O
    1 package 15/° beading needles
    1 pair small sharp scissors
    1 hank bugle beads - either size 3/°
        or 2/°*
    1 hank seed beads - either size 11/°
        or 12/°*
    1 hank contrasting color seed beads -
        either size 11/° or 12/°*
    ----
    * - see "Introduction" for correct
    combination of seed and bugle beads.

The **Bugle Beads** are the foundation for this type of beadwork and serve as a starting point. The number of bugle beads contained in the foundation will determine the width of the finished piece, and will also resolve the overall size of the piece.

Phase I

This phase will form the foundation row of bugle beads that the rest of the piece is attached to. Refer to one of the charted graphs that follow this section and count the number of

9

bugle beads in the chosen design. Join them as
follows:

STEP 1 - Using a single thread (just over
two (2) yards long for an earring six (6) bugle
beads wide), place two (2) bugle beads on the
thread and push them to within 6-8" of the end
(leave enough thread to tie off later), as shown
in **Figure 1** (below).

Holding the short thread down, make a
clock- wise circle with the needle and go "up"
through the first bugle bead following the
direction of the thread **(Figure 2)**. Pull the
thread tight, and the two bugle beads will come
together parallel with each other **(Figure 3)**.

The needle will now be coming "up" through
the first bugle bead. Complete this step by
placing the needle "down" through the second
bead **(Figure 4)**.

STEP 2 - Continue adding bugle beads, one
at a time, following the procedure described
above and shown in Figures 2 through 4.

You will notice that there is a rhythm to
this procedure as it progresses. The thread
will go in a clockwise direction and then in a
counter clock-wise direction, then clockwise
again, etc.

As bugle beads are added, make sure that

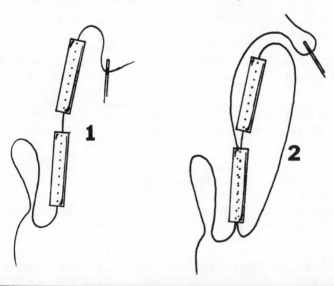

10

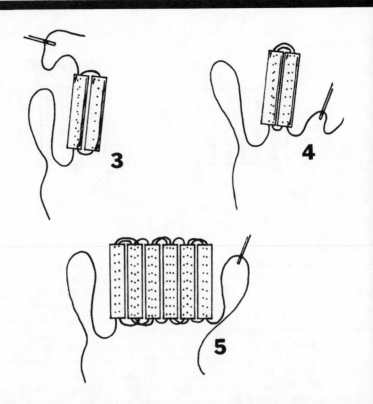

the thread is coming either up through, or down through the last bugle bead, depending upon the direction the thread is going. This can be simplified by **always** keeping the short "beginning" thread facing toward the left and downward (**Figure 5**). This will help lessen any confusion and assist in keeping the proper place.

When the beading thread is in the last bugle bead strung, pick up another bugle bead and, following the course of the thread, go either up through or down through the last attached bugle. For example, if there are two (2) bugle beads attached, the thread will be coming down through bugle number 2. Put bugle number 3 on the needle and go back down through bugle number 2. Now go up through bugle 3. Put on bugle #4 and follow the thread by going back up through bugle #3, then down through bugle 4,

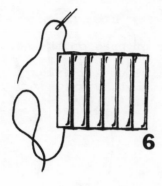

and so on.

As shown in Figure 5, the rhythm for a six (6) bugle bead-wide piece will be: Bugles #1 and #2 on thread (with short thread to the left and pointing down), then up through #1, down through #2 and add number 3; down through #2, then up through #3 and add number 4; up through #3, then down through #4 and add number 5; down through #4, then up through #5 and add number 6; up through #5 and down through number 6.

With all six bugles in place, **work your way back across the bugles to reinforce them.** This is done by going up through #5, down through #4, up through #3, down through #2 and up through #1.

When the required number of bugle beads are in place, **do not cut the thread.** The next phase is the upper portion of the earring and to begin **the thread should always be coming "up" through the first bugle bead** before adding the seed beads. Therefore, the first small bead should always be on the left of the piece. **(Fig. 6)**

Phase II

This phase will form the top portion of the beadwork piece. It is accomplished by adding one bead at a time to the bugle bead foundation just completed.

   STEP 1 - Following the design on anyone of the charts that follow these instructions, place the required color of bead on the needle and pass the needle toward you, under the thread that goes between bugle #1 and #2 **(Figure 7)**. This is easily accomplished by pushing the needle between bugles #1 and #2, and by pulling the needle and thread on through, it will place the bead in position on top of the bugles.

   STEP 2 - To lock the bead in place **(Figure 8)** pass the needle up through the bead. Make sure the needle does not pass under the span of thread again as this will remove the bead from the thread.   With the first bead in place, put the second bead on the thread and pass the needle under the thread between the second and third bugle bead as shown in **Figure 9**.   Then bring the needle and thread up through

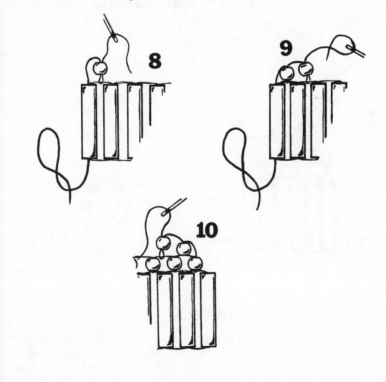

this bead and lock it into place.

Continue this procedure (following the colors on the charts), beading on the first row of beads from LEFT to RIGHT. With the first row of seed beads in place, the needle and thread will be coming up from the bead on the far right. Move up one row on the charted designs to the bead directly above the row just finished. Now following from RIGHT to LEFT, place the proper color beads, one at a time, on the thread using the same procedure as the preceding row, **going under the thread between the seed beads,** rather than the bugles beads as shown in **Figure 10.**

The work on the seed bead portion (Phase II) will continue in a LEFT to RIGHT, then RIGHT to LEFT, then LEFT to RIGHT, etc., manner. As this proceeds there will be one less bead in each row you add. Also, the first row of beads will have one less bead than the bugle bead row **(See Figure 11).** Therefore, an earring containing

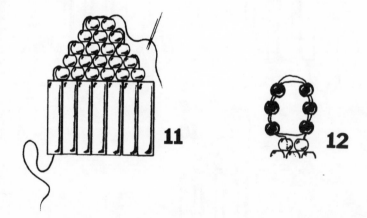

11

12

seven (7) bugle beads in the foundation row (Phase I), will have six (6) seed beads in the first row, five (5) beads in the next row, four (4) beads in row Three, three (3) beads in the next row, and two (2) seed beads in the fifth, or top, row. As the beading is done in this phase, it is easy to see why it is important to use beads that are all the same, exact size.

STEP 3 - When the row having only two beads has been put in place, it is time to add the hanging loop: After locking the last bead in place on the top row, the thread will be coming up out of the bead on the right side in this example of seven bugle beads wide. However, using an even number of bugle beads will result in ending with the thread on the left side. As shown in **Figure 12**, place an even number of beads on the thread (approximately six (6) beads for earrings), go through these beads again and then take the needle down through the other bead on the two-bead, or top, row. Now pull the loop next to the top row.

In larger earrings, as the loop that has been formed will support the piece, work the thread through the same beads again (including the beads in the loop). This will add strength.

Phase III

In this phase the bead dangles will be put in place at the bottom of the beadwork piece.

To do this, work the thread, diagonally, down through the beads to the bugle bead at the starting point as shown in **Figure 13**. With the thread down through the first bugle bead on the left, place the appropriate number and colors of seed beads on the thread (following the chart for the correct number and colors). Add one bugle bead at the bottom of the dangle, as indicated on the charts, and add three (3) seed beads. With the exception of these last three seed beads, pass the needle back up through all of the beads on the dangle; then push the needle back up through the first bugle on the foundation (Phase I) row as shown in **Figure 14.**

Adjust the dangle so that it will hang properly by placing a finger tip over the center bead of the three beads at the bottom of the dangle. By pulling the thread, adjust the dangle so that it hangs properly without too much or too little tension. As the work progresses, it is possible to feel the proper amount of tension.

To progress to the next dangle, pass the needle down through the next bugle bead on the foundation row (bugle bead #2), and add the next beaded dangle following the chart for color and number of beads.

Continue this process until all of the dangles are in place. Make sure that each has been properly adjusted so that they all hang with the same amount of tension.

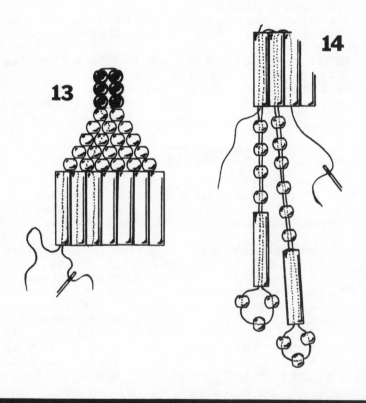

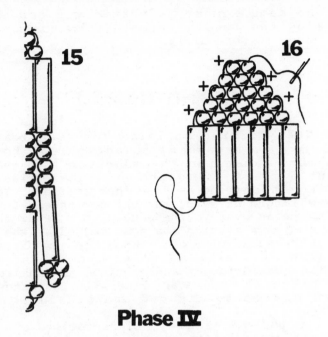

Phase IV

As shown in **Figure 15**, when the dangles have been put in place tie the thread off between two of the rows of seed beads on the outside edge in the top portion of the piece. As shown in **Figure 16**, every other row of beads has a thread on the outside edge and it is desirable to tie two knots just above one of these beads. This way, the thread knots will lie between the beads and when the thread is passed up through additional beads to be concealed, the knot will pull snug against the bead and be less noticeable.

When the thread has been concealed in additional beads, clip it off close to the beads holding the scissors flat against the beadwork. It is suggested when concealing the thread, that after knotting, the thread be woven through beads on the inner part of the beadwork before it is clipped off to insure that the knot does not slip.

After completing this step, then thread the short beginning thread on the needle and tie off in the same manner as just described above: working the thread through a few beads, after knotting, to conceal it.

ADDING THREAD

When working on larger pieces of beadwork it may be necessary to add thread to the project. When the thread being used reaches about 6 to 8" in length, tie it off as when ending an earring as described earlier. To add a new length of Nymo, run the new thread through a few beads over to the edge of the beadwork and tie two knots using the same method as when the old thread was tied off. When the new thread is tied in, weave it up to the point where the beading was left off and continue as usual until the piece is complete. Figure 16 indicates the best places to tie off and/or add the new thread.

It is much easier, of course, to use Nymo of sufficient length to avoid having to add more thread.

BASIC DESIGNS

The following pages contain graphs of some of the basic designs for making beaded earrings using the techniques outlined in the preceding section.

The earring charts are placed in order of difficulty. The first are easy and simple, and those shown at the back of this section are more difficult. The most time consuming designs are those containing quills and those that have patterns in the bottom portion.

It is suggested that craftspersons who are not familiar with this type of beading begin with the simple charts and work toward the more difficult.

Explanation of Graphed Styles

At the bottom of each graphed design there is a "style" noted. The following is a short explanation of each:

Regular Style refers to an earring, or necklace, in which the dangles (Phase III from the last section) taper in the regular "V" shape.

Tapered Dangle Style is an earring, or necklace, in which the dangle tapers in one direction. The dangle graduates from short on one side to long on the opposite side.

Because of the taper to one side, these earrings should be placed on the ear wires so that there is a left and right earring. Having the long side closest to the face seems to be more flattering in most cases.

Inverted Dangle Style refers to a piece in which the dangles taper to an inverted "V" shape. The longest dangles, in this case, will be on the outside.

Loop Style is an earring or necklace in which the dangles are made by looping the beads from one foundation bugle bead across to the corresponding bugle opposite. For example, on a piece that is seven (7) bugle beads wide, the outside, and longest loop, would span from bugle #1 to bugle #7; the second loop would span from bugle #2 to bugle #6; the third loop would span from bugle #3 to bugle #5; and, the center would be a straight dangle from bugle #4 or there would be no dangle from #4, whichever is preferred.

Loop Style is not recommended for use on necklaces as they tend to catch on objects and break more easily than on earrings.

Bead & Quill Style is a piece in which porcupine quills are used in place of some of the beads in the dangles. A section on the preparation of quills is included in this section just prior to some of the charts.

Regular Style Bottom Design is an earring or necklace in which the dangles taper in the regular "V" shape, but also contains a definite "picture" design such as those used in loomwork, needlepoint, cross-stitch or other charted designs.

Top or **Bottom Design Styles** refers to the portion of the beaded piece which contains the design. As noted above, the construction of the top piece was described in Phase II, and the bottom portion in Phase III.

Preparation and Use of
Porcupine Quills

Some of the following charted designs use porcupine quills in place of seed beads. Quills are available from most Indian craft supply houses or it is possible in many parts of the country to gather your own. In the latter case, the following may be helpful.

Porcupines have quills over most of their body, except for the stomach, and they are found below the long guard hair and mixed in with the short body hair. The best earring quills are found on the back from the middle to the tail.

By being selective as the quills are pulled it is possible to avoid getting a large amount of hair mixed in with the quills. The hair will have to be separated from the quills and by eliminating it to begin with, it makes sorting easier and faster.

After the quills are pulled, they can be washed in a solution of 1 part liquid household cleaner and 3 parts water. Put this solution in a spray bottle and, after spreading the quills out on a surface that will drain, spray them liberally. After they have been covered with the solution, rinse them in warm water until the cleaner has been washed off. Another method that works nicely is a plastic container that has a grater lid. Just make sure to use something the quills cannot slip through while washing them.

This procedure is to remove the natural body oils but if they are quite dirty, it may be necessary to wash them again.

If the quills are not going to be used immediately, after they have been washed and rinsed lay them on paper towels or newspaper to dry. The quills, when they are wet, will be flexible but will become firm again once they dry. Keep them separated so that they will dry faster. They may now be placed in an air tight container to keep them from becoming dusty. When it is time to use them, place the quills in warm water for a few minutes to soften them before following the next step.

If, however, the quills are to be used immediately, they are ready as soon as they have been rinsed as they can be cut without splitting when they are flexible. Select the quills largest in diameter and use a guage made from a piece of wire, or a toothpick, to cut a quantity of them to the same length, trimming off both ends. This can be done more accurately if the dark tip is clipped off first and then the length can be cut from the root end of the quill.

After the quills have been cut and have dried to a stage where they will not flatten out, select a long, fine pin with a large head. Quills are not hollow but have a pithy interior. The pin should be pushed through the very middle of this pithy material so that the hole made by the pin cannot be seen from the outside. The hole should be large enough to allow the beading needle to pass through readily without causing the thread to fray or the needle to bend or break. The quills may be cut to any length desired, but must be at least one-half ($\frac{1}{2}$") inch shorter than the beading needle used when making the earrings. If they are longer, it is not possible to pull the needle and thread through them.

By doing several quills at the same time and keeping them in a separate container, it will speed up the beading process when making this style.

‑ ‑ ‑ ‑ ‑ ‑ ‑ ‑ ‑ ‑ ‑

Variations may be made of any of the graphed designs shown in this section by using other kinds of beads, dentallium shells, Russian olive seeds, etc. Simply by changing the colors involved in any of the designs shown, it is possible to change the appearance greatly.

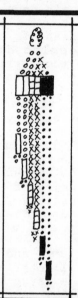

LEGEND

▯ = Gold Bugle

▤ = Bronze Bugle

▮ = Dk Brown Bugle

o = Gold
X = Rust
● = Brown

Diagonal
Stripe Design
Taper Style

PLATE II

PLATE III

Bottom
Cross Design
Regular Dangles

LEGEND

▯ = Black Bugle

● = Black
o = Pearl

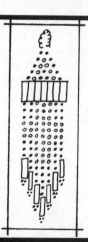

22

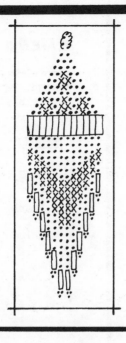

LEGEND

▯ = Red Bugle

● = Black
x = Red

Four Diamond Top, Regular Dangle Style

PLATE IV

PLATE V

Regular Style Bottom Design Earring

LEGEND

▯ = Crystal Bugle

O = White
● = Black
— = Grey
x = Blue

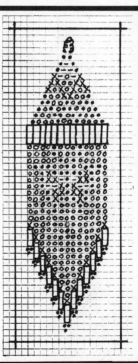

23

PLATE VI

Top Triangle
Design
Inverted
Dangle Style

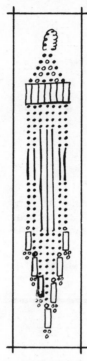

Bottom Cross
Design in
Quills

PLATE VII

PLATE VIII

Top Flower
Design, Taper
Dangle Style

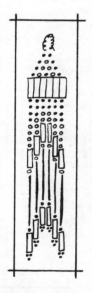

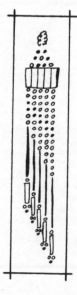

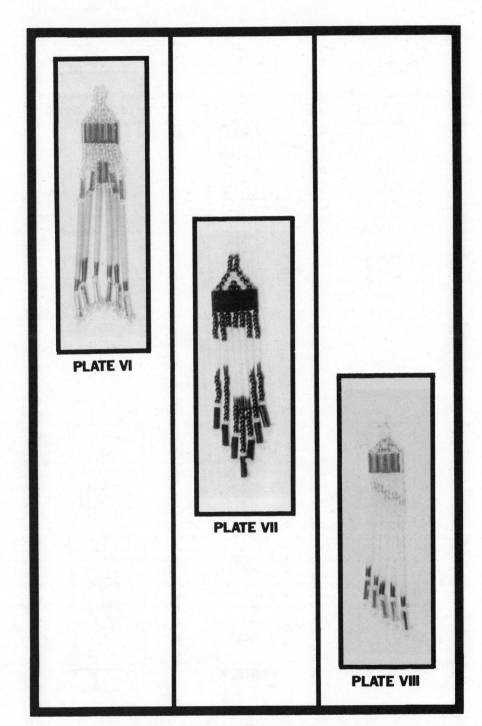

PLATE VI

PLATE VII

PLATE VIII

25

PLATE IX

Diagonal Stripe
Top, Regular
Dangle

LEGEND

▯ = Pink
Bugle

○ = Cheyenne

● = Trans Rose

| = Dyed Quill

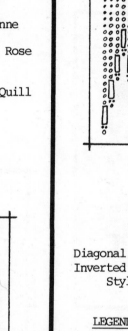

PLATE XI

Top Reversed
Triangle, Regular
Dangle Style

LEGEND

▯ = Dark Green
Bugle

● = Lt Green

X = Dark Green

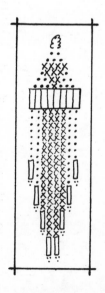

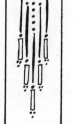

Diagonal Design
Inverted Dangle
Style

LEGEND

▯ = Orange
Bugle

● = Orange
Pearl

○ = Lt Blue
Pearl

PLATE X

26

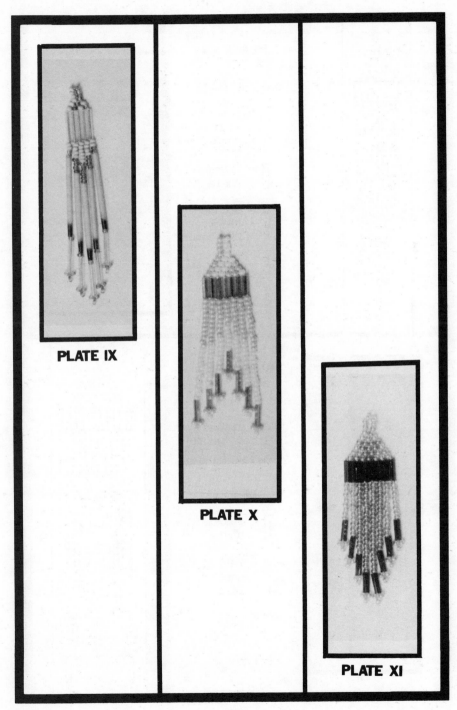

PLATE IX

PLATE X

PLATE XI

27

PLATE XII

Regular Style with Russian Olive

<u>LEGEND</u>

▯ = Orange Bugle

o = Orange Pearl

x = Dk Orange

● = T. Brown

◖ = Olive

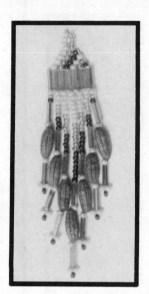

PLATE XIII

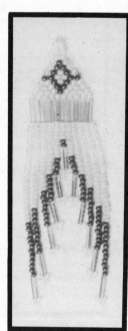

Top Diamond Inverted Dangle Style

<u>LEGEND</u>

▯ = Yellow Bugle

● = Yellow Luster

x = Yellow

– = Rust

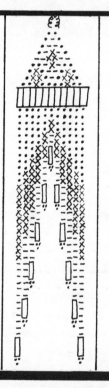

Alphabet Design

Almost any type of alphabet may be used on earrings and necklaces but the letters graphed on these two pages are good examples and show the minimum size recommended (note the picture and graph on Page 31 with an "X". Though attractive as is, the letter would be more distinct if the earring were two beads wider). All of the graphs are for "top design" but the photos/charts show an alphabet design in a "bottom design" earring.

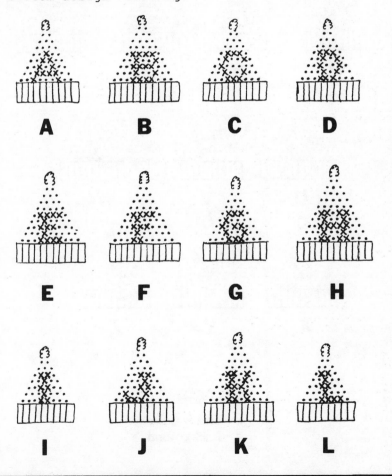

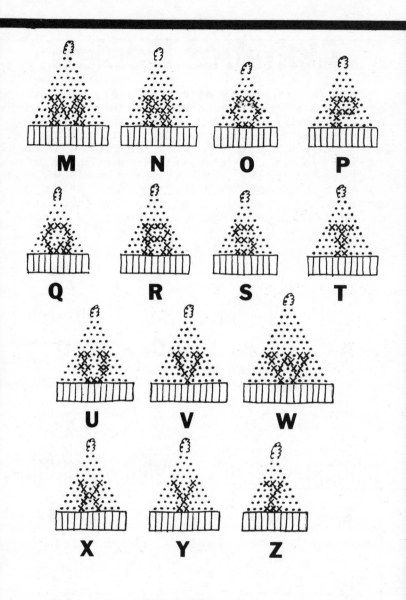

M **N** **O** **P**

Q **R** **S** **T**

U **V** **W**

X **Y** **Z**

<u>**LEGEND**</u>

x = **Letter Color**

● = **Background**

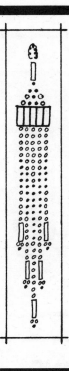

PLATE XIV

Top "X"
Regular Dangle
Design

<u>LEGEND</u>

▯ = Lavender
Bugle

o = Lavender

● = Turquoise

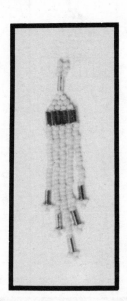

Top & Bottom
Alphabet

<u>LEGEND</u>

▯ = Dk Blue
Bugle

● = White

x = Blue

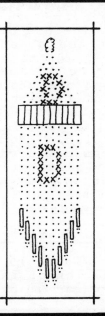

PLATE XV

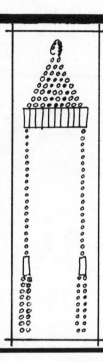

Top "A"
Extended
Loop
Design

<u>LEGEND</u>

▯ = Dk Brown
Bugle

◯ = Root Beer

● = Orange

PLATE XVI

DANGLE VARIATIONS

The use of loops with any design adds another dimension to earrings. In **Figure 17** the "Extended Loop" used above with a "D" alphabet design is shown.

In the photos and graphs that follow in this section, different types of loops are used to create very distinctive earrings that have a regular "top design."

Figure 18 shows how to create a "full loop" design earring with either beads or porcupine quills and **Figure 19** is for the creation of the "Multiple Loop" earring or necklace.

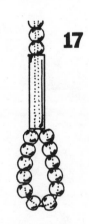

17

Extended Loop

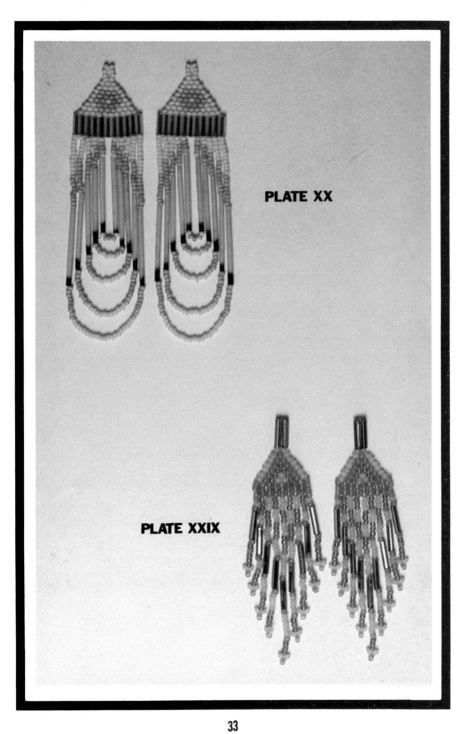

PLATE XX

PLATE XXIX

33

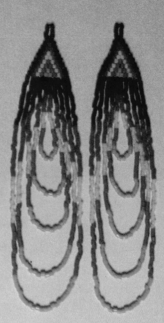

PLATE XXXIII

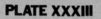

PLATE XXXVI

PLATE XXXXVI

PLATE XXXXVII

35

PLATE XXXXIII

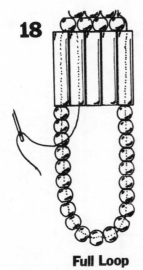

18

Full Loop

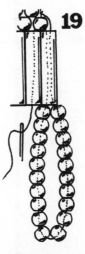

19

Multi-loop

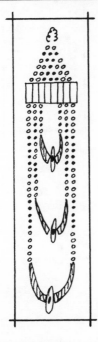

Top Cross
Design, Dentallium
Full-Loop Dangle

<u>LEGEND</u>

▯ = Turquoise
Bugle

○ = Turquoise

● = Turquoise
Rocailles

◣ = Dentallium
Shell

◐ = Disc Wafer
Bead

PLATE XVII

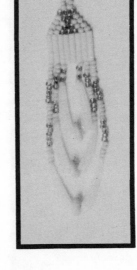

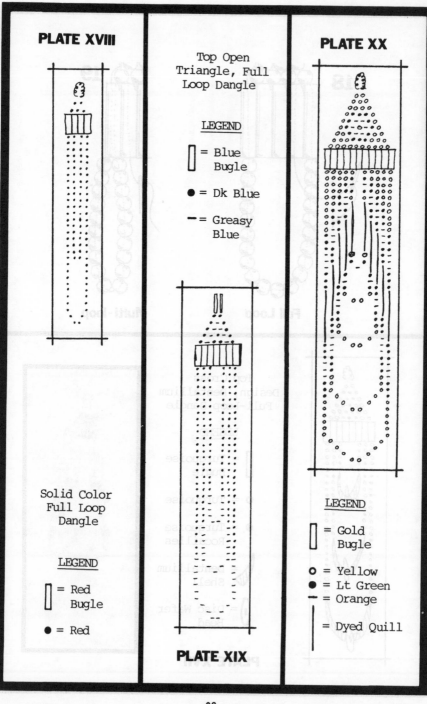

PLATE XVIII

Top Open
Triangle, Full
Loop Dangle

<u>LEGEND</u>

▯ = Blue
Bugle

● = Dk Blue

– = Greasy
Blue

Solid Color
Full Loop
Dangle

<u>LEGEND</u>

▯ = Red
Bugle

● = Red

PLATE XIX

PLATE XX

<u>LEGEND</u>

▯ = Gold
Bugle

○ = Yellow
● = Lt Green
– = Orange

| = Dyed Quill

38

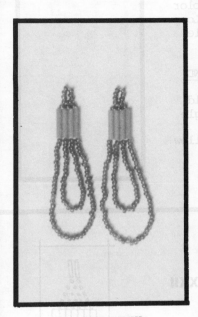

PLATE XVIII

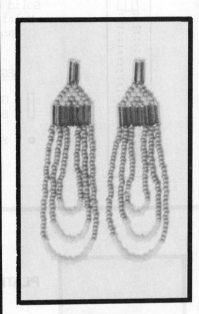

PLATE XIX

PLATE XX

See Color Photo
on Page 33

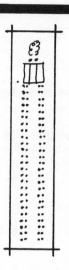

PLATE XXI

Solid Color
Multi-Loop
Dangle

<u>LEGEND</u>

[] = Gold
     Bugle

● = Yellow

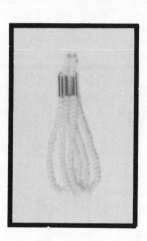

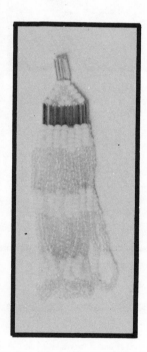

PLATE XXII

Top Triangle
Multi-loop
Dangle

<u>LEGEND</u>

[] = Dark Pink
     Bugle

● = Dark
     Pink
○ = Light
     Pink

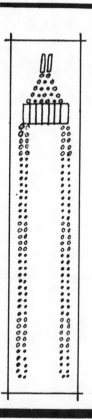

The "multi-loop" dangle, as seen in the photos and diagrams on the facing page and in **Figure 19,** differ from a regular loop only in that it has one full loop per bugle bead in the foundation row. This is accomplished by placing the appropriate beads on the thread and then making the loop by returning up through the same bugle bead. Do this for each bugle bead. Please note that the charts show only the two outside "multi-loop" dangles in order to keep them from being confusing, but remember that each dangle contains the same number of beads in the same sequence as shown on the charts. In other words, follow the sequence shown in the chart for every dangle under the bugle beads.

CYLINDER STYLE EARRINGS

Following the instructions given in this book, make an earring in the usual manner but be sure you choose (or design) an earring with dangles that are all the same length; not one that has inverted or tapered dangles. Before tying the thread off, fold the earring to form a circle with the first and last foundation bugle bead touching. Then pass the needle and thread down through bugle number one and up through bugle seven (or the last bugle bead in the row) as shown in **Figure 20** and **Figure 21.** Do this two or three times for strength. This forms the earring into a cylinder shape. Then tie the thread off in the usual way.

Compare the photo of the earring in Plate 23 with the picture on Page 33 in the first book of **Techniques of Beading Earrings** and it can be seen how different the same pattern can look when made into another style.

Another technique that may be used to make the cylinder earrings unique is the manner in which the cylinder is formed. In Plate 24 the diagram and photo shows an earring with a diagonal stripe in both the top portion and the

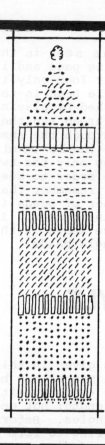

PLATE XXIII

Top Diamond/
Flower Design
Cylinder Style

<u>LEGEND</u>

 = Bronze
Bugle

● = Dk Brown
/ = Rust
— = Yellow

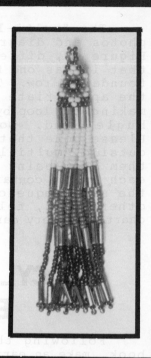

PLATE XXIV

<u>LEGEND</u>

Top Diagonal
Cylinder Style

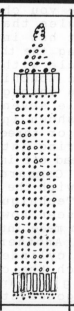

= Purple
Bugle

● = Lavender
○ = Teal
— = Turquoise

20

21

dangles. Both earrings in the set were made exactly the same way but when the cylinder was formed, one earring was folded "inward" (with the first and last bugle beads folded to the front of the earring and tied together). The other earring in the set was folded "outward" (with the first and last bugle bead folded to the back of the earring and tied together. This results in the diagonal stripes going in opposite directions. Of course, if the diagonal stripes are to go in the same direction, both earrings would be folded in the same manner; either inward or outward.

POSSIBLE VARIATIONS

Most of the techniques described in this book may be combined with others to create a combination that is unique and beautiful. The two earrings charted and photographed on the next page are made by using both the "multi-loop" and cylinder techniques.

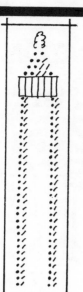

PLATE XXV

Double Stripe Diagonal
Cylinder Style
Multi-Loop

$\begin{bmatrix}\ \end{bmatrix}$ = Green
Iris
Bugle

● = Green

/ = Green
lined
Red

PLATE XXVI

Top Heart Design
Cylinder Style
Multi-loop Dangle

LEGEND

$\begin{bmatrix}\ \end{bmatrix}$ = Dk Green
Bugle

○ = Green
lined
Yellow

● = Dk Green

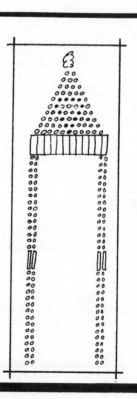

SEED BEAD FOUNDATION

The main difference in this technique and the basic style is that seed beads are used in place of bugle beads to form the foundation row. As shown in **Figures 22 through 26,** three seed beads are used in place of each bugle bead (the complete instructions for Phase I are found on Pages 9-12). When the foundation row is complete, proceed as usual with the creation of the earring.

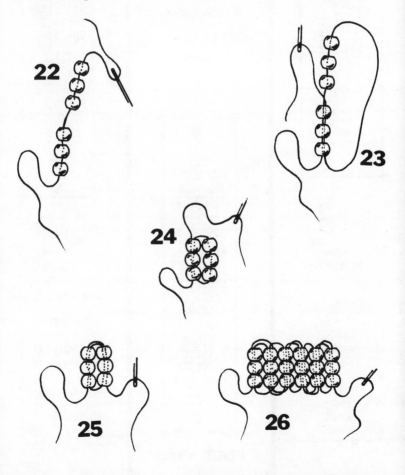

PLATE XXVII

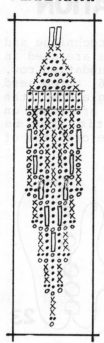

Top Triangle
Regular Dangle

LEGEND

▯ = Gold Bugle

○ = Beige

● = Dk Brown

╱ = Lt Green

Pegan Triangle

LEGEND

▯ = Red Bugle

● = Grey Pearl

○ = Ivory Pearl

x = Trans Red

PLATE XXIX

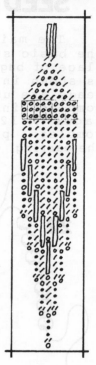

Pegan
Tri Design
Regular Dangle

LEGEND

▯ = Purple Bugle

○ = Lavender

● = Blue

╱ = Lt Green

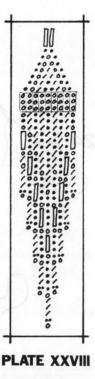

PLATE XXVIII

PLATE XXVII

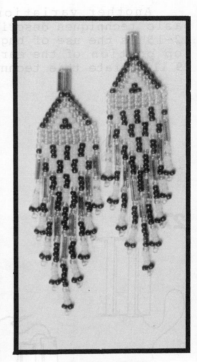

PLATE XXVIII

PLATE XXIX

See Color Photo
on Page 33

BUGLE BEAD PHASE II

Another variation that builds upon the basic techniques described for Phase II on Pages 12-15 is the use of bugle beads to construct the top portion of the earring. **Figures 27 through 29** illustrate this technique.

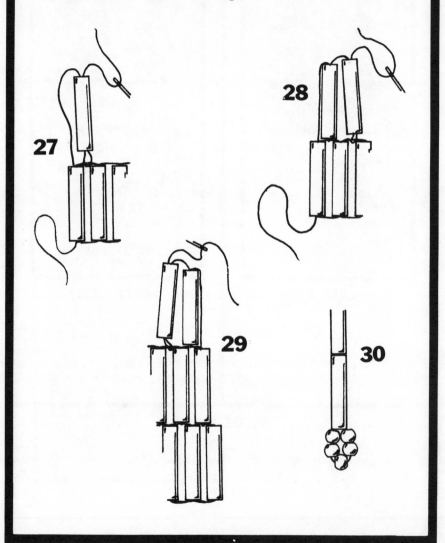

Please note that the earring in Plate XXX features a "full-loop" dangle. In the "Bird Design" in Plate XXXI the foundation row (Phase I) is made of bugle beads but the design is made distinctive with the use of three seed beads in place of one of the bugle beads in the dangles (Phase III); **Figure 30** illustrates the bottom. The earrings in Plates XXXII & XXXIII are made with 15/° Hexigon Beads; the small earrings in Plate XXXII feature an "Extended Loop" and the chart shows only the two outside dangles. The other dangles should be done in the same manner.

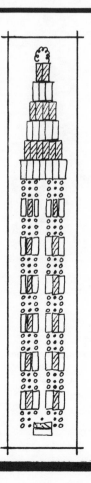

PLATE XXX

Bugle Bead
Full Loop
Dangle

<u>LEGEND</u>

▯ = Red Bugle

▨ = Grey Bugle

o = Red
● = Grey

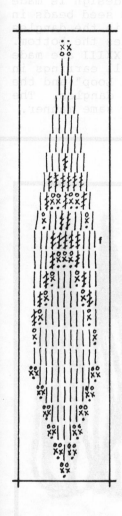

PLATE XXXI

Bird Design Bugle Bead Earring

LEGEND

| = Yellow Bugle

≴ = Red Bugle

o = Yellow

x = Orange

● = Red

f = Foundation Row

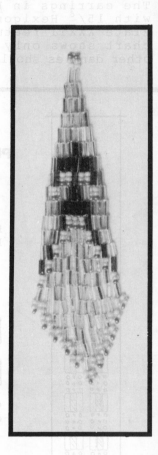

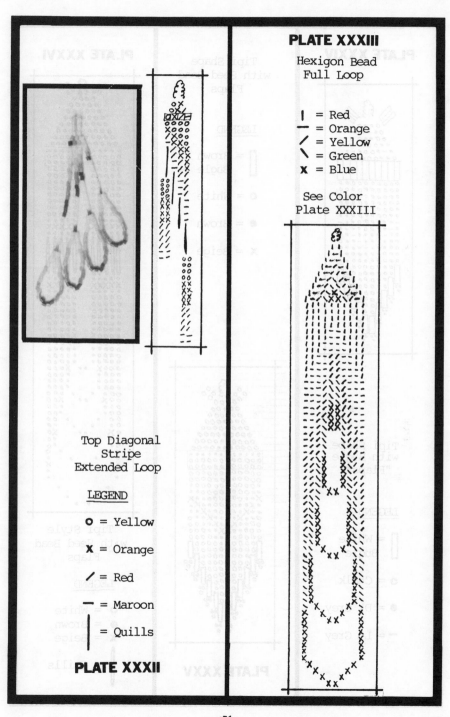

PLATE XXXIII

Hexigon Bead
Full Loop

| = Red
— = Orange
／ = Yellow
＼ = Green
x = Blue

See Color
Plate XXXIII

Top Diagonal
Stripe
Extended Loop

LEGEND

O = Yellow

x = Orange

／ = Red

— = Maroon

| = Quills

PLATE XXXII

PLATE XXXIV

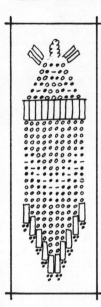

Tipi Shape
with Seed Bead
Flaps

LEGEND

☐ = Brown
     Bugle

o = White

● = Brown

x = Beige

Tipi Shape
with Bugle
"Flaps"

LEGEND

☐ = White
     Bugle

o = Chalk

● = Dk Grey

— = Lt Grey

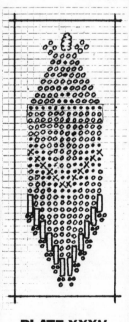

PLATE XXXV

PLATE XXXVI

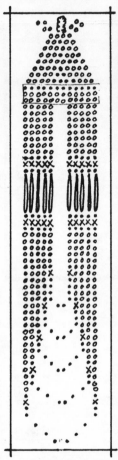

Tipi Style
with Seed Bead
Flaps

LEGEND

o = White
● = Brown
x = Beige

☐ = Quills

PLATE XXXIV

PLATE XXXV

PLATE XXXVI

See Color Photo
on Page 34

TIPI STYLE EARRINGS

As shown, the foundation row of this style earring may be formed with either seed beads or the usual bugle beads. The technique that makes this style unique is the addition of the "smoke flaps."

Make the top portion (Phase II) in the normal way until the row with four beads is reached. As shown in **Figures 31-34**, when this row is completed, place four beads (or two bugle beads) on the thread and go back down through the same bead. Work the thread across to the bead on the opposite side and with thread coming up through the bead repeat this step, going back down through the same bead. To form the hanging loop, work the thread over to one of the center beads and with the thread coming upward add beads of a contrasting color. Form the loop and work the remainder of the earring as indicated in the general instructions.

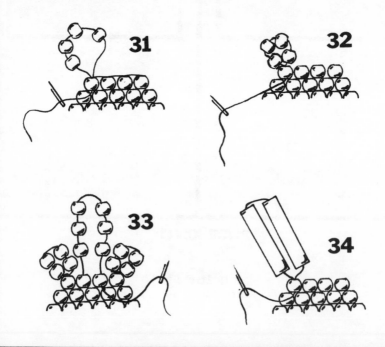

DOUBLE-BEADED STYLE

This is an exceptionally attractive style of earring or necklace and all of the techniques involved are covered in the basics steps.

After the top portion (Phase II) has been completed, turn the piece upside down and repeat the step. However, on this part (the bottom) the beading will include a one-bead row. Now the dangles may be added.

Starting at the one bead row, add the appropriate number and color of beads to form the bottom dangle. Take the needle back up through the bottom bead and then work the needle up until it comes out above the outside bead, on the right side, in the three-bead row. Go down through this bead, add the necessary beads for this dangle and come back up through the bottom of the same bead (**Figure 35**). Then work up until the needle is above the bead, on the right-hand side, in the five-bead row. Continue until there is a dangle on every other row. When the right-hand side has been completed with dangles, work over to the left-hand side and add corresponding dangles.

When all of the dangles are in place, tie the thread off as descibed in Phase IV.

35

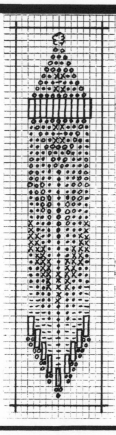

PLATE XXXVII

Double
Beaded

LEGEND

⌷ = Black
    Bugle

● = Black

○ = Red

x = Orange

— = Yellow

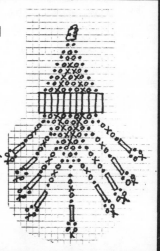

PLATE XXXVIII

LEGEND

⌷ = Blue
    Bugle

● = Blue

○ = White

x = Red

OPEN TRIPLE TRIANGLE EARRING

Begin this beautiful style by making a foundation row (Phase I) in the usual way. When working Phase II, follow the chart examples and make one top portion on the left that includes a one-bead row, then work back down to the foundation row and make a top portion on the right side also. For example, if the foundation is 12 bugle beads wide, the left side top portion will be five beads wide using bugle beads 1 through 6 and the right side will utilize bugles 7 through 12. When this part is completed, another portion is made seperate from this one.

Start by making a secondary foundation row using half the number of bugle beads as in the main foundation row. In the example above, this row would be six bugles wide. When this Phase I is completed, continue with a standard Phase II, that includes the hanging loop, and work the thread back down through this portion to the left side of the secondary foundation row as is usual before adding the dangles.

At this stage the two parts of the earring are combined to form the "Open Triangle." With the thread emerging from the bottom of bugle bead #1 in the secondary foundation row, take it through the top bead in the one-bead row of the left-hand triangle on the main body of the earring. Then work down through the right side of this triangle to the foundation row and then up through the left-hand side of the right triangle and secure the top bead in the one-bead row to bugle #6 in the secondary foundation.

Now work back down into the body of the earring and through the foundation row in the usual manner in order to add the dangles to the bottom of this row. Place the dangles on in the usual manner using regular, inverted or "full loop" dangles to complete the earring.

In a large earring or on a necklace, it is a good idea to make two or three passes between the secondary foundation and the top bead.

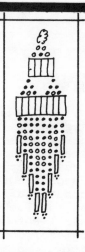

PLATE XXXX

Open
Triple
Triangle

<u>LEGEND</u>

▯ = Red
Bugle

● = Red
Pearl

○ = Ivory
Pearl

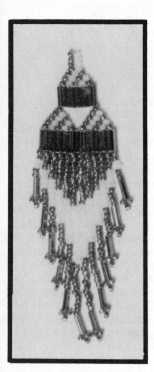

PLATE XXXXI

<u>LEGEND</u>

▯ = Dk Blue
Bugle

● = Dk Blue

○ = White
Opal

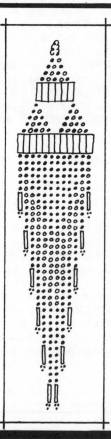

NECKLACE
&
LOOP

All of the necklaces in this section may be made with the following recommended materials:

1 bobbin "nymo" thread size A or O
1 package 15/° beading needles
1 pair small sharp scissors
1 hank bugle beads - either size 3/°
    or 2/°*
1 hank seed beads - either size 11/°
    or 12/°*
1 hank contrasting color seed beads -
    either size 11/° or 12/°*
----
* - see "Introduction" for correct combination of seed and bugle beads.

Making the body of the necklace is done by following the steps in the first section, Phases I through IV, and the variations. As shown in the following charted graphs, the techniques are the same but they are simply made larger.

In order to attach the body of the necklace to the necklace chain, it is necessary to make a "hanging loop strip." You use the same method in creating the hanging loop strip as was used for making the top portion of the beadwork (Phase II), with one exception, which comes in attaching the second bead of each row.

The first bead of each row of the hanging loop strip will be put in place in the usual manner used in Phase II of the earring section as shown in **Figure 36.** The two dark beads in all of the following figures indicate the top row of the beadwork in the necklace piece.

After the first bead has been put in place in the usual manner, string a second bead on the

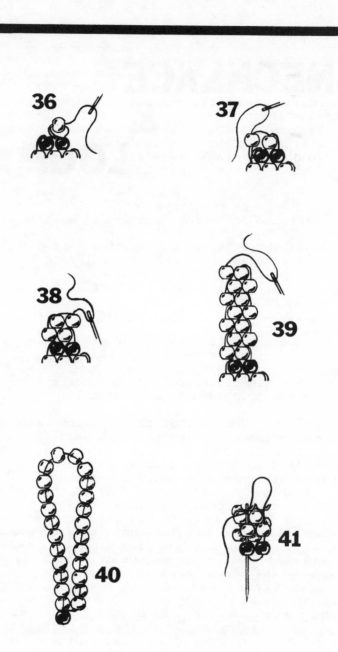

thread and pass the needle under the thread lying on the outside edge of the bead in the preceding row as shown in **Figure 37**. The remaining rows will be put on using this same technique **(Figure 38)**.

Figure 39 shows seven rows of the hanging loop strip; note the "zig-zag" pattern.

For an average necklace, the hanging loop strip will contain approximately twenty-four (24) rows of beadwork, two beads wide. This length will allow almost any size beads used on the bead necklace chain (explained below) to easily pass through the hanging loop when it is completed.

To form the hanging loop from the 24 row strip now constructed, fold the strip over until the two beads in the last row of the strip are directly in front of the two beads in the top row of the necklace piece. **Figure 40** is a side view of the loop now formed. Fasten the hanging loop by passing the needle down through the bead on the top row of the necklace body **(Figure 41)**, then up through the other bead at the top of the necklace body, up through the corresponding bead at the end of the hanging loop strip and repeat this procedure two or three times for strength.

You are now ready to work the thread down through the necklace body in order to add the dangles (Phase III), or if the thread is too short, tie it off, and tie in a longer one (as explained in the earring section).

<<<<<<<< * >>>>>>>>

It should be noted that this section of instructions, for making the hanging loop, are written with the thread emerging from the bead on the **right hand** side of the top row in the necklace body. However, if a necklace is made in which the thread is coming from the bead on the left side, the only difference is that the first row will be worked from left to right rather than right to left. The number of bugle beads contained in the foundation determine from which of the two top beads the thread will emerge. Using an uneven number of bugle beads will place the thread on the right hand side of the top row; whereas, an even number of bugles will place the thread on the left side. In either case, the final results will be the same.

Also, if the body of the necklace is very large (e.g., the butterfly pattern pictured on the front cover), it will help make the body more sturdy by running additional thread through the beads as done when going down from the top to the dangles.

The following are graphs and photos of some necklace bodies that may be made from these instructions:

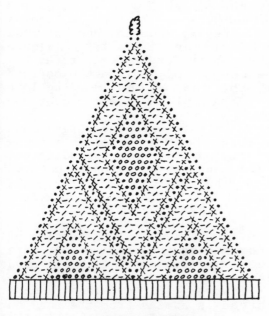

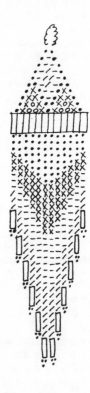

PLATE XXXXIII

Top of Necklace and Earring Graph
See Page 63 for "Legend"
Color Photo on Page 36

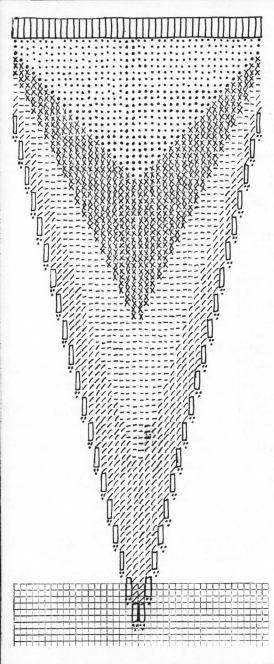

PLATE XXXXIII

All-Over Diamond
Necklace & Earring
Set

LEGEND

⎕ = White
    Bugle

● = Black

○ = White

✕ = Burgandy

— = Turquoise

╱ = Orange

<<<< * >>>>

Top of Necklace and
Earring on Page 62

Color Photo on
Page 36

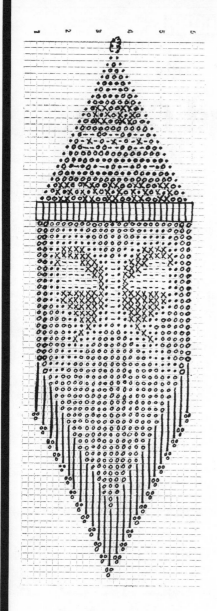

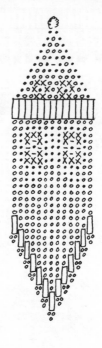

Butterfly Necklace and
Earring Set

(Photo on Front Cover)

<u>LEGEND</u>

⬜ = Brown
Bugle

● = Brown
○ = Beige
X = Orange
— = Turquoise

| = Quill or
Long
Bugle
Bead

PLATE XXXXIV

Necklace

Bead Chain

In order to secure the necklace around the neck, it is necessary to make a "chain" in the following manner:

Recommended Materials Needed

1 Spool Size 12 Tigertail Wire
2 Crimp beads (either gold or silver colors)
1 Pair small needle nose pliers
1 Spring-type necklace clamp
1 6mm Jump Ring (either gold or silver)

First determine the desired length of the necklace chain. An average length for a "chain" is approximately eighteen (18") inches. To allow for attaching the crimp beads, add about two (2") inches to the desired finished length. For example, to make an 18" chain, the tiger tail should be approximately 20" inches long.

After the tigertail has been cut to the desired length, slip a crimp bead over one end and position it about one (1") inch from the end. Put a jump ring over the same end following the crimp bead. Now take the short end of the tigertail over the jump ring and through the crimp bead to form a loop; allow the jump ring to hang free in the loop just formed. When the loop is adjusted, squeeze the crimp bead closed with the pliers (See **Figure 42** for a view of the loop).

Now string the beads on the tiger tail, in any desired pattern, to within approximately one inch from the end of the tigertail. The photos shown in this book will give some good examples of patterns that may be used but the variations are endless.

When the pattern is acceptable, slip the other crimp bead over the 1" end of the tiger tail. Now put the tigertail through the small ring of the necklace clamp, fold the tigertail over and go back through the crimp bead and close it with the pliers. This step finishes the bead chain.

Attach the necklace portion to the bead chain by sliding either end of the chain through the hanging loop.

It is important to have the two halves of the necklace chain correspond in pattern by having the same number of beads on each side. If there is to be a "center pattern" that will vary from the rest of the chain, it is recommended that you begin the chain by putting the center pattern on the tigertail first, sliding it to the middle and then add one pattern of beads at a time; working first on one side, then on the other until approximately 1" remains on both ends. Then add the crimp beads, jump rings and necklace clasp as above.

The only difficult part of the center pattern technique is keeping the beads from sliding off of one end while the loop is being made on the opposite end. The open end may be secured with an "alligator clip," by holding it in your teeth or by finding a "helping hand."

Keep in mind that the possible variations that may be used in making the necklace chain are almost unlimited and that beads make of glass, wood, ceramic, metal, etc., may be used. The only requirement is that they have a hole big enough to allow the tigertail to be used and that the beads be small enough to go through the hanging loop.

Plate 45, on the next page, shows some of the necklace chains that may be made.

42

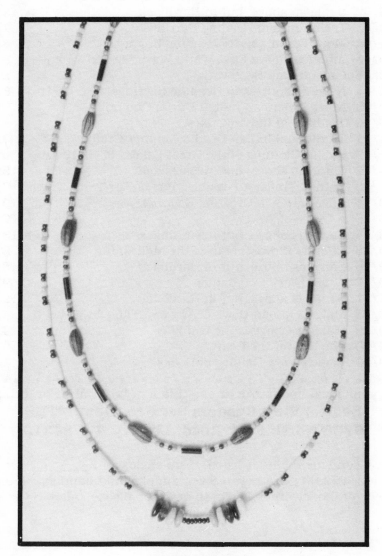

PLATE XXXXV

SOME BEST SELLING BOOKS FROM EAGLE'S VIEW

B00/01	Techniques of Porcupine Quill Decoration...	$8.95
B99/01	Same as above, but in Hardback	15.95
B00/02	Techniques of North American Indian Beadwork	9.95
B99/02	Same as above, but in Hardback	15.95
B00/03	Techniques of Beading Earrings	7.95
B00/04	More Techniques of Beading Earrings	8.95
B00/05	America's *First* First World War: The F&I War	8.95
B00/06	Crow Indian Beadwork	8.95
B00/07	New Adventures in Beading Earrings	8.95
B00/09	North American Indian Burial Customs	9.95
B00/10	Traditional Indian Crafts	8.95
B00/11	Traditional Indian Bead & Leather Crafts	9.95
B00/12	Indian Clothing of the Great Lakes: 1740-1840	9.95
B99/12	Same as above, but in Hardback	15.95
B00/13	Shinin' Trails: A Possibles Bag of Fur Trade Trivia	7.95
B00/14	Adventures in Creating Earrings	9.95
B00/15	A Circle of Power	7.95
B99/15	Same as above, but in Hardback	13.95
B00/16	Etienne Provost: Man of the Mountains	9.95
B99/16	Same as above, but in Hardback	15.95
B00/17	A Quillwork Companion	9.95
B99/17	Same as above, but in Hardback	15.95
B00/18	Making Indian Bows & Arrows...The Old Way	9.95
B00/19	Making Arrows...The Old Way	4.00
B00/20	The Hair of the Bear	9.95
B00/00	Eagle's View Catalog of Books	1.50

• •

At your local bookstore or use this handy form for ordering:
Eagle's View Readers Service, Dept MTBE
6756 North Fork Road, Liberty, UT 84310

Please send me the titles listed. I am enclosing $_____ which includes $2.00 per order to cover shipping and handling. (Send check or money order - no cash or CODs please. Allow 3 weeks for delivery.)

Ms./Mrs./Mr. _____

Address _____

City/State/Zip Code _____